IS IT POSSIBLE FOR SENIORS TO AVOID A FALL?

Antonio E. Morales-Pita, Doble PhD

authorHOUSE®

AuthorHouse™
1663 Liberty Drive
Bloomington, IN 47403
www.authorhouse.com
Phone: 833-262-8899

Published by AuthorHouse 07/29/2023

ISBN: 979-8-8230-1197-6 (sc)
ISBN: 979-8-8230-1196-9 (e)

Library of Congress Control Number: 2023913840

In memoriam to my mother Siria,
whose example as tenacious has inspired my life forever.

To my late wife Gladys, whose remembrance and extraordinary love
keep making of me a better man.

Contents

INTRODUCTION

"**Most important thing in life is learning** how to fall."
Jeannette Walls, Half Broke Horses

"**We all die. The goal isn't to live forever, the
goal is to create something that will.**"
Chuck Palahniuk

FALLS ARE THE leading cause of injury, emergency room visits, and hospitalizations for seniors in North America. Every eleven seconds, an emergency room in the United States sees a senior fall victim. Falls can reduce independence and accelerate the need for long-term care. The good news is that one can reduce the risk of falling with simple exercises that anyone can easily learn, **as long as** the readers are tenacious enough to learn the exercises, to practice them systematically, and to enjoy them.

When somebody suffering from a physical issue falls and attends a physical therapist, he/she can learn how to avoid a fall. This is the first indispensable part, but there is a second part that hardly appears in bibliography, **namely the necessary inclusion of tenacity as part of the exercises.**

This writer explored the paper "Testing Ways to Encourage Exercise", done by the National Institute on Aging, Research Highlight.

Reading the paper, this writer copied some important information about this exercise:

"Fewer than one in four adults in the U.S. get the amount of exercise recommended to maintain health and prevent chronic disease. Designing interventions that encourage people to exercise more regularly has proven challenging."

"Research has tested many strategies to increase physical activity. But these studies tend to be small. Variation in populations, locations, and other factors also makes it hard to compare results. And what works in one setting may not work in another"

"To overcome these limitations, researchers led by Drs. Katherine Milkman and Angela Duckworth from the University of Pennsylvania tested dozens of different ways to boost exercise using a novel approach they developed called a mega study. The research team included thirty scientists from fifteen universities. They enrolled more than 60,000 members—with an average age of about forty twenty-four hours of Fitness gyms, a national fitness chain. Members are required to check in electronically before using the gym. This allowed the researchers to track how often people exercised before, during, and after the study.

Five of the interventions stood out for being especially effective. One provided higher overall rewards for workouts. Two provided bonus rewards for returning to the gym after a missed workout. One let participants choose whether they wanted their rewards framed as losses or gains. And another one sent text messages informing participants that most Americans exercise, and that this fraction is growing.

To explore the value of the mega study approach, the researchers surveyed more than three hundred experts in the field about which programs they thought would most effectively boost exercise. Those predictions did not match up with the interventions that resulted in the most gym visits.

'These results show how difficult it is to predict which interventions to increase exercise will work,' says Dr. Duckworth. 'They also highlight the value of mega studies, Milkman adds, which allow researchers to test many different approaches to changing behavior at once in order to determine what interventions are most effective.

Negative results from small studies often get little to no attention. Mega studies have the additional advantage of being able to rule out, all at once, many interventions that don't work. They're now being used to test other public health interventions, such as encouraging vaccination".

At the end of the day, the scientific group could not get definite conclusions. An interesting factor to point out is that the word tenacity was not mentioned in the previous scientific study. Sometimes, it is taken for granted that lack of tenacity is a factor that interferes in the basis of these partial results.

In this author's opinion, if human beings were tenacious in undertaking of this scientific magnitude, the results would have had better trends. This author understands that tenacity is very difficult to measure through scientific indicators, but **the purpose of this paper is to underline the importance of tenacity as an important factor that may at least partially influence the lack of continuity of exercising once the treatment is over.**

This author is a highly tenacious man; therefore, he continues reaping good results of all his physical training sessions. As a conclusion, the sessions are not the end of the exercise, but just the beginning. For the last two years he has received three physical therapy sessions with three different physical therapists, and combines the exercises from the three. On top of that, he can feel the huge difference in the outstanding results by daily walking at least two miles, (according to his iPhone results). During the months of July and August 2022, he has been walking more than 2.5 miles per day.

Tenacity allows him to get over somewhat temporary lack

of enthusiasm to continue. He is enjoying how his muscles are getting stronger

Food For thought

1. Does the reading of this chapter make you aware of the importance of exercising?
2. Can you **comprehend** why the word "tenacity" is not included in most books to successfully strengthen the body through exercising.
3. Why do they concentrate in creating exercises without mentioning the word "tenacity"

CHAPTER I

Literature Related To Falls For Seniors

"Sometimes it takes a good fall to really know where you stand"
Hayley Williams

Balance and Your Body, by Amanda Sterczyk

*H*OW *EXERCISE CAN help you avoid a fall*, by Amanda Sterczyk, who is a fitness professional

The writer of the book is a fitness professional, whose literary creation is meant to help the reader to improve his posture and to understand why and how to do the exercises.

The book is divided into three parts: the problem (fear of falling, exercise vs getting in shape, balance and gravity); the solution (fall prevention, balance basics, balance and strength, balance and posture, balance and your joints; and finally the action plan (functional fitness, and the exercises).

It contains many exercises preceded by a scientific explanation as follows: In the first part the book analyzes fear of all exercise vs. getting in shape, and balance and gravity. In the second part the book deals with fall prevention, balance basics, balance and strength, balance, and posture, as well as balance and your joints. The third part goes deeply in more than 25 different exercises comprising the whole body.

This is very good book, to which this author will go every now and then to interiorize the need to exercise. He is highly motivated to exercise, especially after being prognosed with stenosis in his neck and some other parts of my vertebral column in 2020. So far in two years he has taken physical therapy with three specialists, he has learned how to improve walking, and to protect him from falling.

From the book this author has taken some recommendations and applied them to his life. Here are some numbers:

In relation to exercising: The book states 150 minutes/ week recommended by the Canadian Physical Activity Guidelines.

This author, in a normal week since 2020 (my first PT after learning of my health problem) I do three types of exercising: **the first one** for the balance : 25 minutes per day times 7 days in a week: 175 minute; the **second one** for strong exercise (30 minutes for the elliptical + 30 minutes for the stationary bike) 60 minutes times 3.5 days in an average week = 3.5 X 60 = 210 minutes; and the **third one:** walking 1.25 miles = 40 minutes X 7 days per week = 280 minutes

In total 175 + 210 + 280 = 665 minutes per week.

On top of that, every day he sits down and stands up ten times without any help, which he complements by standing up three times from the floor.

Getting in and out of a chair without help : everyday ten times; getting in and out from the ground: three times

This author is highly motivated to exercise, and this book is a very good source of improving his balance and his health.

Comparing Ms. Sterczyk's book with mine, I observed that her book assumes that the readers are highly motivated and are tenacious individuals who will consistently introduce the exercises into their lives. The word tenacity is not mentioned at all, despite the fact that, without it, the continuation of the treatment is not guaranteed.

There was no word whatsoever to the motivation to exercise, to continue exercising in a systematic way. This author has written and published several books, like *Grit+Tenacity+Proactiveness* (Holding the Bull by the Horns) which directly leads to include tenacity as a condition to succeed in materializing these exercises, as well as to overcome procrastination, which may preclude the systematic exercising, and consequently to avoid falls.

Consulting google, the author found descriptions of two books: about The book How To Prevent Falls is based on Dr. Betty Perkins-Carpenter's unique Six Step Balance System, designed to teach seniors how to prevent falls and avoid potentially devastating injuries, while increasing energy and maintaining independence through a series of safe, easy and fun to do balance exercise activities.

Another consulted book in this same topic was Better Balance for Life: Banish the Fear of Falling with Simple Activities Added to Your Everyday Routine by Carol Clements

In the search for books, this author never found the word "sense of purpose".

From wordhippo.com, sense of purpose is defined as the action or state of focusing all of one's attention or energy on something.

In this author's book *May Empathy Lead to Sense of Purpose through Tenacity?* on page xii, he cited a very good definition of sense of purpose in Dr. William Damon book's A Path to Purpose, dedicated to analyze this condition on young people, as follows: sense of purpose is a stable and generalize intention to accomplish something that is — at the same time — meaningful to the self and consequential for the world beyond the self."

This author is a prolific writer, whose sense of purpose has experienced some variations through his life. During his early childhood and early youth his sense of purpose was to concentrate on studying primary and secondary education plus the learning of the English language. During his twenties, his sense of purpose was to become bachelor's in economics, professor, and master. During his thirties and forties, he became PhD twice. Therefore, his sense of purpose was to be highly educated, to become a scholar, and professor. He retired after his wife's decease and became a prolific writer dedicated to continuing teaching through his books. On top of that, he became polyglot in Spanish, English, Russian, Italian, and French.

In a summary his sense of purpose was to achieve high professional level as an economist, a professor, a scholar, and prolific writer. His self-defined legacy is and will be to continue teaching through his books. He found the way to perpetuate his sense of purpose after his death.

Thanks to his mother and inborn nature God gave him the talent of being tenacious. Without being tenacious, he wouldn't have been able to overcome innumerable difficulties, which never stopped him in his goal of teaching. For him to write books and to be an inspirational speaker is to continue his passion for teaching. He never said "no" to himself whenever he faced obstacles, for example, to finish his first PhD overcoming procrastination through the opposition of his peers. His frustration didn't stop him, so he looked for and met a Soviet scholar in his specialty (economic cybernetics), who helped him finish and defend his dissertation in Kiev to become a PhD. This author is a prolific writer, whose sense of purpose has experienced some variations through his life. He had to go through four pre-defenses in Havana and Kiev. After positive results of overcoming procrastination on several occasions, right there the day of defending his first dissertation, he started to get ready for his second PhD. Had he not been tenacious, he wouldn't ever had become PhD. His tenacity didn't allow him to give up despite the huge obstacles he faced.

Food for thought

1. Can the readers perceive which is this author's main contribution to the topic of avoiding falls?
2. Why most books mention exercising, but not tenacity?

CHAPTER II

Health Consequences of Falling for Seniors

"There is a fountain of youth: It is your mind, your
talents, the creativity you bring to your life and
the lives of people you love. When you learn to tap
this source, you will truly have defeated age."
Sophia Loren

"Time is not measured by the passing of years but by what
one does, what one feels, and what one achieves."
Jawaharlal Nehru

CONSEQUENCES OF FALLS in the elderly include **hip fractures**, especially among women, who have an 18% risk of getting a hip fracture in their lifetime. The risk of hip fractures is higher in seniors who have porous, fragile bones (osteoporosis).

The following information and data were taken from https:// www.onhealth.com › seniors' falls, and fractures

"Hip fractures are unfortunately common in older adults, and dementia increases this risk. Osteoporosis often develops as people age and so bones are less likely to remain intact in a **fall**. **Falls** are the cause of 95% of hip fractures, and 75% of those hip fractures occur in women.

The risk of **hip fracture** rises with age. **Risk** increases because bones tend to weaken with age (osteoporosis). Multiple medications, poor vision and balance problems also make older people more likely to fall — one of the most common causes of hip fracture.

A hip fracture is a serious and yet common outcome when an older adult has a fall. It occurs due to the progressive decrease in bone mass that often affects women and men as they age. Another risk for hip fracture is osteoporosis, a skeletal disease marked by a loss of bone density, which leaves bones porous, thin and brittle.

Because of the hormonal changes that occur during menopause, women are at increased risk of developing osteoporosis. (Although it's more common in women, men can develop osteoporosis, as well). These skeletal changes are reflected in hospital records, which show that more than 300,000 adults over the age of 65 are admitted each year due to a hip fracture, nearly all the result of falling, usually sideways.

Unfortunately, it's true that a hip fracture in older adults can contribute to poor outcomes, including an increased risk of death. A number of factors play a role. These include the age of the patient, their sex, and the health problems the person was living with before the fracture, such as cardiovascular, pulmonary, or neurological issues; diabetes; declining cognition or frailty.

Most hip fractures in older adults require surgery to restore mobility and to manage pain. This puts patients at risk for a range of post-surgical complications, including infection, blood clots in the lungs or legs, bedsores, urinary tract infection and pneumonia. Recovery for adults who are older or frail can take months. This often leads to further loss of muscle mass, which then increases the risk of a subsequent fall. Due to the length of recovery, a hip fracture also often leads to a decrease in independence.

Following surgery, many patients are surprised to learn that physical therapy starts almost immediately. It's an important part of the recovery process. Not only does physical therapy help patients regain mobility, but it also helps prevent the more serious complications associated with being immobilized, such as infection, developing a blood clot or pneumonia. Proper nutrition, with adequate protein, also plays a role in recovery. So does occupational therapy. It keeps the patient mentally and emotionally engaged, and can lessen the risk of depression.

One factor that can go overlooked, particularly among older adults, is pain management. It's crucial to an optimal recovery. Make sure your grandmother's pain levels are being clearly communicated, and that her health care providers are responding appropriately. It's useful for her to think of pain in terms of a scale of 1-to-10, and important for her to communicate to her doctors and nurses what she is experiencing.

Unfortunately, many older adults won't return to their same level of activity and independence following a hip fracture. Your family should be prepared to decide to get your grandmother the future help she will need.

Falls account for 87% of all **fractures** among **people** aged 65 years or **older**. For **seniors, fractures** are the most serious consequence of **falls** (short of death). The most common **bones** to fracture in **falls** are: The **hip**, femur (thigh **bone**), pelvis, and vertebrae (spine); the humerus (upper arm **bone**), forearm, and hand; the leg and ankle **bones**."

Food for thought

This author recommends the readers to think about possible answers to the following three questions:

1. What is the main reason why falls in seniors are so much more dangerous than in non-seniors?

2. How can a senior improve his probability of not falling without damaging his/her body?
3. Is it possible for a senior beyond 80 or even 90 not to fall? Under what premises or circumstances can he/she be able to avoid falling?

CHAPTER III

U. S. Statistics about Seniors' Falls

"How people die remains in the memory of those who live on"
Dame Cicely Saunders.

"Our dead are never dead to us, until we have forgotten them"
George Eliot.

"It is natural to die as to be born"
Francis Bacon.

T HE READERS ARE recommended to go through the first two tables of this chapter along with their conclusions, and to try to figure out if they can add their own conclusions to the third one.

Table #1 Statistics about Senior tables. Taken from https://wisqars.cdc.gov/fatal reports

From Google, The **crude death rate** is the ratio of the number of **deaths** in a geographic area in one year divided by the average population in the area during the year. The age-specific **death rate** is the ratio of the number of **deaths** occurring in a specified age group to the average population of that group.

Age group	Sex	Year	Metro areas	# deaths	Population	Crude rate
60-64	**Males**	2010		612	6.64 million	9.21
		2015		781	7.54	10.31
		2020		1,015	8.37	12.12
	Females	2010		279	7.275	3.83
		2015		371	8.33	4.45
		2020		550	9.141	6.08
65-69	Males	2010		587	4.741	12.38
		2015		634	6.240	14.97
		2020		1231	6.940	17.73
	Females	2010		373	5.404	6.90
		2015		501	7.0	7.10
		2020		706	7.9	8.89
70-74	Males	2010		844	3.7	24.77
		2015		1,130	4.3	26.24
		2020		1,706	5.6	30.45
	Females	2010		609	4.1	14.82
		2015		791	2.1	15.49
		2020		1,207	6.6	18.29
75-79	Males	2010		1,231	2.5	47.79
		2015		1,572	2.9	53.81
		2020		2,127	3.6	57.89
	Females	2010		1,051	3.8	31.06
		2015		1,249	3.7	33.65
		2020		1740	4.6	37.89
80-84	Males	2010		1,757	1.8	93.90
		2015		2,131	1.9	108.1
		2020		2,728	2.2	121.04
	Females	2010		1,855	2.8	65.27

		2015		2,092	2.8	74.89
		2020		2,636	3.1	85.38
+85	Males	2010		3,631	1.5	246.15
		2015		5,213	1.8	289.41
		2020		6,623	2.0	328.52
	Females	2010		5,813	3.0	190.57
		2015		7,940	3.4	233.09
		2020		9,670	3.5	272.09
TOTAL				329,526	734 million	444.87

Conclusions from the table:

The crude rate for males from 2010 to 2020 grew from 9.21 to 10.31, an increase of 31%.

The crude rate for males from 2010 to 2020 grew 31% in the ages 60 to 64, 43%; in the ages 65-69, 27%; in the ages 70-74, 23%; in the ages 75-79, 21.1%; in the ages 80-84, 28.9%; and in +85, 33.3%.

In the period from 2010 to 2020, there are three trends in the crude rate for males: a) ascending from 31 to 43 in the ages from 60 to 69; descending from 27 to 23 to 21 in ages 70 to 79; and ascending from 21 to 29 and 33.3 60 to 64, from 79 to 85.

The crude rate for females from 2010 to 2020 show two trends: a) descending from 58 to 29, to 23, to 22 in the ages from 60 – 64 to 65 – 69, to 70 – 74, to 75-79; and ascending from 22 to 31 to 42 in the ages from 80-84 and +85.

Table # 2 Comparison male – female crude rates in each age category in 2020

Age group	Male (range)	Female (range)	Range male/female
60-64	9.21 to 12.12	3.83 to 6.08	12.12 / 6.08 = 1.99
65-69	12.31 to 17.73	6.9 to 8.89	17.73 / 8.89 = 1.99
70-74	24.77 to 30.55	14.82 to 18.29	30.55 / 18.29 = 1.67
75-79	47.79 to 57.89	31.06 to 37.89	57.89 / 37.89 = 1.52
80-84	93.90 to 121.04	65.27 to 85.38	121.04 / 85.38 = 1.41

| +85 | 246.15 to 328.52 | 190.57 to 272.09 | 328.52/ 272.09 = 1.20 |

From table # 2 the following conclusions can be derived:

a) From ages 60 to 69, the crude rates in the U.S in males was the double of that in the females.

b) As ages start to increase, the crude rates in males/ females started to go down from 1.67 in the group 70-74 to 1.2 in the group +85.

Average age of retirement for men and women in the US Crude rate:

What is crude death rate in the US?

Number of deaths over a given period divided by the person-years lived by the population over that period. It is expressed as number of deaths per 1,000 population.

Table # 3 – Death rates in the US

Infant mortality rate	5.69 deaths/1000 live births
Under 5-mortality rate	6.98 deaths/1000 live births
Adult mortality rate	Deaths/100
Age 15-50	8.48
40+	94.19
60+	80.98
Female adult mortality	13.42
, in the Male adult mortality	22.08
Number of deaths	2,960.99
Idem age 0-24	331.08 thousand
"25-69	4,647.89"
"70+	9,174.47"
Number female deaths	6,860.11

Life survivors at age 25	98,428
Life survivors at age 70	77,571

Falls Are Serious and Costly

Facts About Falls (cdc.gov) Graph # 1

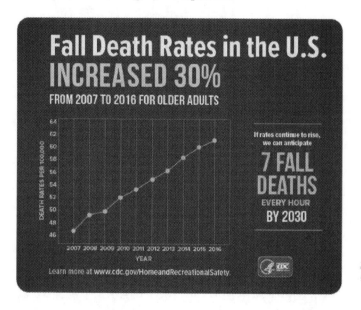

- One out of five falls causes a serious injury such as broken bones or a head injury[4,5]
- Each year, 3 million older people are treated in emergency departments for fall injuries.[6]
- Over 800,000 patients a year are hospitalized because of a fall injury, most often because of a head injury or hip fracture.[6]
- Each year at least 300,000 older people are hospitalized for hip fractures.[7]
- More than 95% of hip fractures are caused by falling,[8] usually by falling sideways.[9]
- Falls are the most common cause of traumatic brain injuries (TBI).[10]

- In 2015, the total medical costs for falls totaled more than $50 billion.[11] Medicare and Medicaid shouldered 75% of these costs.

It is interesting to that, despite the influence that exercising has on the falls, and consequently, on the death rates, it is not registered in the data so far presented in www.cdc.gov/Homeand RecreationalSafety.

I also read 10 Best Practices for Staying Healthy at Age 60, by Kendal at Oberlin, which I summarize herein:

1. "Eat healthy, 2. If you drink, do it in moderation, 3. Stay fit and maintain a healthy weight, 4. Get enough sleep, 5. Get regular health screenings and vaccinations, 6. Make your home safe, 7. Learn something new, 8. Socialize, 9. Engage on the internet, 10. Cultivate a positive attitude."

In all the consulted bibliography, I have noticed that it is taken for granted that the person attempting to cover the ten practices, must be tenacious.

Consequently, my contribution to attempt reducing falls – and consequently death– is to emphasize <u>the importance of continuing exercising after the sessions with professional technicians are over</u>. In other words, the body requires systematic exercising as part of elderlies' lives. It is necessary, but not only, to include and to create useful exercises to avoid falls, it is – I repeat – indispensable to incorporate exercises into the patients' lives.

As an important conclusion, it is in the patients' hands to continue independently on their own. After receiving the necessary treatment with PT, if they want to save their lives, not to be a number in the list of fall death rates in the US, they must wide open develop their tenacity, stand up after a fall, and to reject procrastination. So, whenever, disappointment, lack of enthusiasm, sadness, tiredness, hesitation, hesitation is trying to be present in your lives, reject them through your iron will.

Stand up and say good-bye to depression, sadness, fears. All of them won't be able to resist the power of tenacity.

Celebrate your triumphs against procrastination. Keep exercising thru the thick and thin. When you start feeling the positive effects of exercising according to your professional trainers' instructions, you would be in the first stage of the process. Keep on, and very soon you will see and feel the good results.

As an example of my own life. In the fall of 2020, I started the first serious training with an expert PT. When I finished the last session in December 2020, I have kept exercising every day. The second training specifically oriented toward balance, took place in January 2021. Instead of stopping the 2020 exercises, I added them to the new ones. In July 17, 2022, I started my I third training that will be over on August 4th.

This last training has positively changed my life for the following reasons:

1. I have added walking one mile per day to the exercises. Now I am walking with my cane on the floor; in other words, I am walking permanently holding my dear friend the cane, but not with it on the floor. I already surpassed the face of walking holding the cane on the floor. Keeping a regular pace, never running, never trying to catch up with other pedestrians, I walk with the assurance that I will not fall.

2. It took me two days to start writing a book about avoiding falls for seniors. It is incredible how my hands are accepting the challenge of finishing the manuscript at the latest on August 30th, 2022.

3. I am full of enthusiasm, courage, sure to have overcome the possibility of falling being 82 years old, because my brain has wholeheartedly accepted the challenge of incorporating exercising as part of my sense of purpose.

4. Now I feel in control of my health.

Food for thought

1. The readers are recommended to read this chapter again.
2. What is the main purpose of including this chapter into the book?
3. Do you feel prepared to defeat procrastination through a reiterated passion of continuing exercising?
4. Have you self-assigned goals of incorporating systematic exercising into your everyday life?
5. When you already feel the benefit of exercising through a) increased strength in your muscles, and b) safety of walking without the fear of falling, please jot down the date.

CHAPTER IV

Falling is the Most Dangerous Enemy of Living Longer

"Lack of activity destroys the good condition of every human being, while movement and methodical physical exercise save and preserve it"
Plato

"Most important thing in life is learning how to fall."
—*Jeannette Walls, <u>Half Broke Horses</u>*

Don't Fall For It!
By **Christine Gulotta, DPT, Director Of Memory Care At The Larsen Pavilion Skilled Nursing Facility, Shell Point Retirement Community**

D ID YOU KNOW that one in four older Americans falls every year?

Falls are the leading cause of both fatal and nonfatal injuries for people over 65 years old. Those numbers double for seniors with visual trouble or deficits. This is because visual impairment adversely affects perception of environment and the surrounding elements that can cause a fall.

However, low vision is not the only contributing factor to tumbling over; your overall physique and daily activities play a role too. Understanding the signs and causes of falling is half the battle.

Here are some common factors that can lead to a fall:

- **Balance and gait:** Loss of coordination, flexibility, and balance is a natural part of aging. This can occur primarily through inactivity, making it easier to fall.
- **Vision:** In the aging eye, less light reaches the retina, making contrasting edges, tripping hazards, and obstacles harder to see.
- **Medications:** Some prescriptions and over-the-counter medications can cause dizziness, dehydration or interactions with each other that can lead to a fall.
- **Environment:** Making modification in your apartment as removing all rugs, bright lights, and pathway obstructions can reduce some risk.
- **Chronic conditions:** Condition like diabetes, stroke, or arthritis often increase the risk of falling because they result in lost function, inactivity, depression, pain, or multiple medications.

Although I agree with the first five factors leading to a fall, although there is one factor that is hidden inside the balance and gait.

Let me explain myself. Loss of coordination, flexibility and balance can be measured using scientific methods but only exceptionally through statistical data. They are hard to quantify because their components are hard to isolate; that is to say, loss of coordination most likely will imply lack of flexibility (but again, how to measure flexibility parameters)

The remaining four components are subject to be quantified; namely, **lack of vision** through optical instruments, **medications** are widely studied in this country and they are easy to quantify. For example, four months ago I fell apparently due to some lack of coordination in my brain. I went to the Emergency Room of Northwestern Hospital in Chicago; they subject me to several tests, including analysis of my brain. Incredibly fast, in less than three hours, they discovered that the reason of my fall was not in my brain or in my muscles. The reason for the high blood pressure (that damaged my health was a medicine whose dosage was increased 25 to 50 mg tablets almost one year ago). The medical team decided to stop this medicine, and substitute it by amlodipine 10 MG. My blood pressure went to normal levels in less than six hours.

Environment is subject to modifications of physical things like rugs, bright lights and pathway obstructions. Finally **chronic conditions** like diabetes, stroke or arthritis increase the risks of falling, but again their individual impact on falling is extremely hard to measure.

In conclusion it is extremely difficult to determine how any of the five factors is more directly causing falls.

Being an inborn tenacious man, I can detect that lack of exercise or inactivity is in direct relationship with falls. At the same time, lack of exercise is caused by lack of tenacity, or procrastination of postponing exercising. In my paternal family there were three persons who were tenacious, two of them never fell and died at 88 years old still healthy. Both precipitated their deaths due to physical mistakes. I am the third tenacious person in good health, who has been exercising for decades, although since the last two years, I have increased the number of weekly minutes of exercising from 400 to 700 or 800. I have self-assigned the goal of walking one mile per day since the last two months, I systematically use my cane holding it in the air, and not on the ground. I am almost 82 years old.

My brother and my youngest sister after turning 50 years old stopped exercising. My brother died at 90 years old, but his last five years were laying on bed most of the time. My youngest sister stopped exercising since she was sixty, and is still alive at 86. My eldest sister died last year at 89, but she stopped exercising after turning seventy.

All physical therapists who have treated me for several years taught me exercises, which I had never stopped doing. Why? Because I am tenacious. Not every day I feel like exercising, but I say to myself: "Common on, Antonio. You cannot miss a single day." I am always adding new modifications so I can never get bored. I am enjoying how my muscles are getting stronger by observing and even increasing repetitions or adding some modifications.

To be able to learn and to feel how much better I am doing reinforce my systematic execution of exercises. I feel sure that I am doing all I can to avoid falling.

This entry was posted in **Fitness**, **Health**, **Long Term Care**, **Preparedness**, **Safety**, **Wellness** and tagged **balance issues**, **causes of falling**, **dont fall for it**, **Fall Prevention**, **Falls are the leading cause of injury**, **physical therapy**, **reduce falling**, **remove obstacles**, **safety**, **stay healthy**, **visual impairment** by **Christine Gulotta, DPT, Director of Memory Care at The Larsen Pavilion skilled nursing facility, Shell Point Retirement Community**. Bookmark the **permalink**.

Try New Things

By **Heather Battey, Resort Services And Wellness Manager, Shell Point Retirement Community**

As we age, we may become reluctant to try new things. Some people are set in their ways or uncomfortable trying a certain food, hobby, or exercise routine that they aren't used to. While it's good to know what you do and do not like, it's important to focus on the many positive benefits of trying something new.

This author will include three factors that can help in avoiding falls for seniors, according to his own experience, that is to say,

1) <u>Is Physical Exercising Possible for Seniors 60 to 85 years old?</u> My answer is yes because I am 82 years old and I have been exercising during my whole life, especially after turning 70. Being retired as a professor at 76 years gave me more time to exercise every day.

2) <u>Is It Possible to Introduce Happiness, Optimism, and Tenacity into Seniors 60 to 85 years old?.</u> My answer is unmistakably yes. I have always loved to sing since I was a young man. I was always singing to my girlfriends. Having said so, when my extraordinary wife died, and I sang at the church the song that was the symbol of our going steady in our youth, I have become a singer in public paying homage to her. I wake up every day singing songs that I learned when I was a boy. Consequently, the more I sing, the happier and more optimist I become every morning. My worst enemy is stress; but my best friend in defeating it singing.

3) *Is It Possible to Introduce Reading Physical Books into seniors 60 to 85 years old? Since I am a prolific writer, whose legacy is to continue teaching through my books, of course I am able to promote reading with the books in the readers' hands.*

Food for thought

1. If the reader is a senior, are you still exercising? *If so, do you exercise every day?*
2. Have you introduced happiness into your exercises? Have you been able to establish a connection between happiness and healthy body?
3. Do you know the difference between being old and feeling old? Being old is a natural process, but feeling old depends upon the senior him/her self.

CHAPTER V

Senior Choice between Tenacity and Procrastination in the Process of Avoiding Falls

My physical **body may be less efficient and less beautiful in old age. But God has given me an enormous compensation: my mind is richer my Soul is broader and my wisdom is at a peak. I am so happy with the riches of my advanced peak age that, contrary to Faust, I would not wish to return to youth." ~**
Robert Muller

"Action will destroy your procrastination."
Og Mandino.

"My advice is to never do tomorrow what you can do today. Procrastination is the thief of time."
Charles Dickens.

S MALL INTRODUCTION ABOUT data related to seniors' falls in the U.S.

According to /www.cdc.gov/injury/features/older-adult-falls/index.htm.

"Every second of every day, an older adult (age 65+) suffers a fall in the U.S.—making falls the leading cause of injury and injury death in this age group. One out of four older adults will fall each year in the United States, making falls a public health concern, particularly among the aging population."

About 36 million falls are reported among older adults each year—resulting in more than 32,000 deaths.

Each year, about 3 million older adults are treated in emergency departments for a fall injury.

One out of every five falls causes an injury, such as broken bones or a head injury.

Each year at least 300,000 older people are hospitalized for hip fractures.

More than 95% of hip fractures are caused by falling—usually by falling sideways.

Women fall more often than men and account for three-quarters of all hip fractures.

After taking note of the preceding threatening data, this author presents some possible solutions related to falls.

Suggestions of Possible Ways for Seniors to Avoid Falling derived from the author's commitment and dedication to improve his health.

1. Strengthening muscles in legs, arms, waist, knees, hip; improving posture, reducing or eliminating back pain; avoiding drooping shoulder by means of an experienced physical therapist's indispensable instructions help, collaboration and participation.
2. Systematic physical exercising.
3. According to this author's experience, tenacity may be improved conscientiously.

4. Some of the reasons why some patients do not continue exercising, shortly after finishing their training sessions –– even with highly experienced empathetic physical trainers–– is due to their lack of tenacity.

5. It is very hard for physical trainers to follow up with their patients. Some patients may even return a year after having concluded their physical training because their pains returned. It is the patients' absolute responsibility to take care of their health. If they are tenacious, it would be easy for them to continue exercising on their own. The ghost of procrastination may introduce lack of enthusiasm, encouragement, sadness, depression, doubt into peoples' brains. The worst enemy of procrastination is tenacity. It is as if tenacity were a guardian against these harmful postponing actions.

6. **According to Wikipedia, Procrastination** is the action of unnecessarily and voluntarily delaying or postponing something despite knowing that there will be negative consequences for doing so. The word has originated from the Latin word *procrastinatus*, which itself evolved from the prefix *pro-*, meaning "forward," and *crastinus*, meaning "of tomorrow."

7. This author suggests readers to motivate themselves to continue exercising by the introduction into their minds of music, excitement, finding fun and encouragement through a thorough analysis of the improvement.

8. Adding tenacity and empathy to yourself, or also to a group of friends.

9. Introducing optimism and love into exercising.

10. Including a cane into your walking habits. Do not regret showing your need to be helped by a cane. It is much worse to fall because the individual was ashamed to show his need for a cane.

11. As times goes by, one can walk holding the cane in your hands always, but not always with the cane pressing it on the floor.

12. Challenge yourself to slowly walking with the cane for at least half-a-mile per day.

13. Enjoy celebrating your victories over pessimism, frustration, defeat.

14. Avoid physical falling completely whenever the enthusiasm dwindles, stand up with your tenacity.

15. Be in control of your health, by attempting to feel how your organs react when pain, or any sign of possible sickness emerge. As soon as possible, look for an appointment or contact your medical doctors to be sure that you are on the right track for being healthy.

16. Never say "no" to yourself. Do not hesitate to spend more money in your health. Avoid sicknesses that were avoided by expeditious visits to specialists.

17. Strengthening muscles in legs, arms, waist, knees, hip; improving posture, reducing, or eliminating back pain; avoiding drooping shoulder by means of an experienced physical therapist's indispensable instructions, help, collaboration, and participation.

18. Practice systematic physical exercising.

19. According to this author's experience, tenacity may be improved conscientiously.

20. Some of the reasons why some patients do not continue exercising, shortly after finishing their training sessions — even with highly experienced empathetic physical trainers— is their lack of tenacity.

21. It is very hard for physical trainers to follow up with their patients. Some patients may even return a year after having concluded their physical training because their pains returned. It is the patients' absolute responsibility to take care of their health. If they are tenacious, it would be easy for them to continue exercising on their own. The ghost of procrastination may introduce lack of enthusiasm, encouragement, sadness, depression,or doubt into peoples' brains. The worst enemy of

procrastination is tenacity. It is as if tenacity were a guardian against these harmful postponing actions.

22. **According to Wikipedia, Procrastination** is the action of unnecessarily and voluntarily delaying or postponing something despite knowing that there will be negative consequences for doing so. The word has originated from the Latin word *procrastinatus*, which itself evolved from the prefix *pro-*, meaning "forward," and *crastinus*, meaning "of tomorrow."

23. This author suggests readers to motivate themselves to continue exercising by the introduction into their minds of music, excitement, finding fun and encouragement through a thorough analysis of the improvement.

24. Adding tenacity and empathy to yourself, or also to a group of friends.

25. Introducing optimism and love into exercising.

Is it easy to become tenacious? Some personal examples of my own life can show that ––if you are decided and convinced of the convenience of going to a medical doctor as soon as you feel that your health is threatened by a sickness–– you are able to start being tenacious.

During the last two weeks I was witnessing some swelling in both legs and some leg cramps. After the first two days I tried to make an appointment with my podiatrist. He was very busy, and the soonest I could materialize the appointment was yesterday (ten days after). I had prepared some written questions to him. Well, he prescribed an arterial doppler bilat, and answered all my questions. I learned that my health issues were not serious; he prescribed me some walking exercises meant to decrease the inflammation and pain. Had I waited for more weeks, then my problem would have necessarily worsened. Therefore, I started to watch the inflammation and learned how to reduce it. I was tenacious! I didn't allow procrastination to stop or to delay my actions.

This is an illustration how tenacity had helped me to overcome procrastination on two occasions.

A) Learning English

At this point I should mention a circumstance that shows the impact my mother had on my student life. I was enrolled at the Havana Business Academy, which was widely known for its educational strictness in assigning students to different levels of English based on their level of vocabulary, grammar, reading and writing skills. I had to do an exam of vocabulary. My level of preparation was so low that I had to guess on multiple choice quizzes. I ignored most of the words, but I had a sort of guessing feeling that indicated to me which answers were right. As a result, I was placed in a level that was higher than the one I was really at. The academy principal was so surprised by my grade on the exam that she offered to my mother —who accompanied me in this adventure — the possibility of placing me in a lower level if I felt that level six was too high for me. The higher the initial level, the sooner I would finish my studies and that was in line with my mother's objectives. Therefore, she told the principal that she trusted in my academic capacity and intelligence. During the first two weeks the pressure was enormous on my brain — of course I did not know, then, that I would be facing harder challenges soon, and that this effort would prepare me — but I never gave up. Whenever I consulted my mother's opinion — when I resisted standing up after a fall – or when I felt overwhelmed by the number of difficult tasks I had undertaken, her answer was always, "Listen, my son, prepare your mind always to go ahead, never backwards, You always must demand extra effort from yourself to grow and to succeed. Do not ever, ever, give up." As a result, I never felt defeated, and always finished whatever I had started. What a way to positively influence my student life and performance!

The conclusion of this application of tenacity into my learning English was that I finished two years of learning English, learned English at an acceptable level, became bilingual stenographer at 16 years old, and got my first job as secretary of the general manager of El Mundo newspaper

My largest proof of having learned English was that at 17, as a tourist I spent 29 days in the United States. I understood everyone I met, and they understood me. I didn't speak one word in Spanish.

This trip was also an example of the consequence of being tenacious because, receiving a salary of $110 per month, in one year I was able to save $500. When I returned to Havana in 1958, I spent the last dollar and visited Miami, Miami Beach, Washington DC, New York, and some cities in New Jersey. I didn't let procrastination to stop my first trip abroad.

B) The challenge to enter at the University of Havana without finishing High School

At the time, I was working as a bilingual correspondent for a governmental exporter of tobacco and its byproducts. (By then the Cuban regime had been declared socialist by Fidel Castro shortly after the Bay of Pigs invasion, and all businesses were taken over by the government.) Because I had a certain prestige for being a serious and responsible student, I was asked by the human resources officer if I wanted to study economics. Inasmuch as the authorities knew I was in my fourth year of high school; I thought the officer was talking about taking an academic course. I said that it was OK because to learn something new was always useful. One month later I was told that I had been selected to study for the bachelor's degree of economics at the University of Havana.

I felt confused. On one hand, my dream was to study at the University of Havana, even though my vocation was not totally defined. Although nobody in my whole family had ever gone to college, I felt the deep need to do it, but in the right way, after being duly prepared. On the other hand, I felt very well placed as a student in "my bachillerato," and I knew it was not right to skip two whole years and enter the university pushed by "patriotic pressures." I protested the decision of the Human Resources Department because

I never thought about interrupting my bachillerato. I kept saying that it was irrational to skip two whole years. To "persuade" me, they appealed to my patriotism and love for Cuba. They kept repeating, "Cuba needs you as an economist. You cannot deceive the confidence we have invested in you." My thoughts wandered somewhat: "Maybe they are right. Maybe I am selfish. I should think about my country's needs. Maybe Cuba cannot wait two years for me to start a career. But the five-year bachillerato is based on the knowledge required to start college. If I start two years earlier, I may have voids in my knowledge. Wasn't this like building a seven-story house without the fourth and fifth floors? Shall I be able to understand college mathematics without the immediately preceding pre-college algebra? Would my brain be ready to undertake the college academic rigor without having finished the pre-college level completely?" Anyway, I was morally obliged to drop the bachillerato and to enter college just like that. The Cuban Revolution history is full of forced movements, done under political pressure and full of occasions in which to say no, was equivalent to being "a bad Cuban."

So, there I was in front of the famous eighty-eight step stairwell of the University of Havana, ready to attend the first meeting of 600 students to start an economics degree in Cuba. The Dean of the College of Economics let students know that the majority of the 600 students had been chosen by officials at their workplaces to study at the University of Havana without having finished the bachillerato. What a big mistake, I thought. So, I was not the only one. Most of those young men and women had not finished pre-college and were obliged to enter the University. Given the assumption that the Secretary of Education had been chosen by such an intelligent man as Fidel Castro himself, I was probably wrong. From an academic point of view, maybe I was right; but, from the point of view of the needs of my country – which Fidel was supposed to know about much better than I – the decision to accelerate the entrance to college should be a good one. At the time, I was working eight hours per day up to five o'clock in the evening and studying for my bachillerato every weekday after leaving my office. From that point on, I would be studying the bachelor's degree in economics instead, but also at night.

The Dean of the College of Economics announced that same night that all students would have to do a placement test in mathematics, and that some pre-college math levels would be established to help those students who could not start the degree when qualified only in college algebra. The placement test would take place twice, the first night for those students who had finished the bachillerato, and the second night for most students who had not finished pre-college. So, there I sat in a huge classroom along with several hundreds of candidates, with a math placement test before me. Some twenty minutes after the test started, the proctor said that if any student wanted to begin with exercises in elementary algebra, he/she could turn in the test blank. I was shocked by the fact that most of the candidates opted to deliver the test blank and to start with elementary algebra. Apparently, the general level was low. I wanted to do my best so that I could start at the fourth year of the bachillerato math level. I preferred not to start with elementary algebra again. So, I tried hard to answer as many questions as possible. I remembered to leave in blank those questions that pertained to trigonometry, which was unknown to me. The results and the different groupings would be announced one week after the exam.

An unexpected event shook me up during the second general meeting of students with the Dean. The academic officer solemnly announced that the results of the tests were so poor that, except for twenty-eight students, the remaining 572 examinees had been placed at the elementary algebra level. I felt deeply aggravated. "Oh my God! To start elementary algebra again," I thought. I was on my way to leave the auditorium when the Dean read the names of the twenty- eight students, and I stopped when I heard my name. No, it could not be. I could not be among the twenty-eight students who are going to start at the college math level. I clearly had written that I did not know trigonometry or other pieces of advanced algebra. Most likely I did not hear well. Just to make sure, I waited until the end of the brief informative assembly and approached the Dean to verify that my name had been included in the special group. The Dean confirmed that I was on the list. I argued with the Dean that there had been a mistake because I had not finished the bachillerato and that I had left blank three of the eight questions. The Dean referred me to the math instructor, an old man in his sixties or seventies. I introduced myself to the instructor. He greeted me in a nice way and asked me what he could do for me. I replied that a mistake had been made in my case because my name was included in the special group, and I had not had enough math education. The instructor stared at me defiantly and said, "There is no mistake. You are in the group." I tried to insist that this was not possible, and then he simply told me, "Antonio, don't be stubborn. I look forward to seeing you tomorrow in the first class." I was really taken aback. Not only was I forced to leave the bachillerato and enter the University skipping two years, but I was also obliged to start with the college-level math. When I returned home, I spoke with my mom. She simply comforted me by saying, "I know you will make it. Simply try hard, as you have always done. You are the first member of our family to get to college, so you have become our role model. Go ahead and never give up. Thanks to the Revolution, you will study college for free. You know what you must do."

The first month of classes was a real challenge. I thought I was going to go nuts. I was obliged to skip two whole years of mathematics and to have a four-week review covering the mathematical stuff of the fourth and fifth year of the bachillerato. I took my classes in shorthand, studying only mathematics. After the second month of classes, I had "acquired" enough experience to go on to calculus. That was the biggest educational challenge I had encountered in my life so far, which led me to knockout procrastination for a second time.

Is it possible to introduce tenacity in seniors who had not used it frequently? My answer is yes for the following reasons:

a) By means of tenacity ––if they finished a set of PT treatment ––, at first, they felt the joy of being healthier at least for some days.

b) Secondly, If they practice the twenty five suggestions listed at the beginning of this chapter –– and they keep on doing them for at least two month –– they might be encouraged to continue feeling well; and very especially, they should have the opportunity of avoid falls.

c) Thirdly, if they continue exercising, and adding joy to the exercises, creating new ones, introducing initiative to feel proud of their achievements, they might recognize improvement in their health issues.

d) Fourthly, do not let procrastination debilitate your joy of improving your health.

e) Never say "no" to exercising, inventing temporary excuses.

f) For male readers, exercising should be conquered as if it were a lady. You can't stop pretending her until she is part of your lives. For female readers, exercising should be encouraged by perceiving improvements in their beauty. According to my 82-year experience, ladies need to feel they are beautiful, while we prefer to be strong.

g) Do your best to say "yes" to tenacity, and "no" to procrastination.

h) Our most cherished victory is to achieve success in our health by introducing tenacity in your lives.

i) The option is yours. Never say "no" to yourselves as far as supporting tenacity and rejecting procrastination.

Additional recommendations

1. To start exercising systematically and as soon as possible.

2. Practice "standing up" .First step. Sitting down on a chair, stand up without any help. Little by little, increase the number of standings up. Second step. Sitting on a mattress stuck to the floor, stand up at the beginning with some help being on the alert about not falling. With the continuation of repetitions, you should be to stand up without any fall.

3. Identify yourself, your muscles, your inner self, your conscience. Be proud of standing up after a physical or psychological fall.
4. Don't ever feel defeated if mistakes start to come your way. We are human beings; and, therefore, are prone to make mistakes.
5. Celebrate on your own terms your small victories against procrastination.
6. Don't ever allow pessimism to grip on yourself.
7. Try to control your reactions or emotions, especially during or after a stressful situation.

Food for Thought

1. Are readers motivated to be tenacious after reading this chapter?
2. Have readers defeated procrastination at least once in their lives?
3. Readers are asked to analyze if they ever started exercising, but then little by little they stopped doing. Some months later they had a fall. Did they feel encouraged (not frustrated with the defeat) but ready to start embracing tenacity?

CHAPTER VI

To be in Control of your Health

The greatest test of courage on earth is to bear defeat without losing heart. In every adversity there lies the seed of an equivalent advantage. In every defeat is a lesson showing you how to win the victory next time. If you learn from defeat, you haven't really lost.
Robert Green Ingersoll

**Famous phrases about optimism and
courage to stand up after a fall**
But man is not made for defeat. A man can
be destroyed but not defeated
Ernest Hemingway

Never confuse a single defeat with a final defeat
F. Scott Fitzgerald

Defeat doesn't finish a man, quit does. A man is not finished when he's defeated. He's finished when he quits.
Richard Nixon

In every adversity there lies the seed of an equivalent advantage. In every defeat is a lesson showing you how to win the victory next time
Robert Dollier

We are not interested in the possibilities of defeat. They do not exist
Queen Victoria

Remember you will not always win. Some days the most resourceful individual will taste defeat. But there is, in this case, always tomorrow – after you have done your best to achieve success today
Maxwell Maltz

THIS IS THE first time in my writing history that I initiate a chapter with famous people's seven phrases especially in the relationship between being tenacious and able to control one's health. The reader is asked to meditate what is the common quality in each one of them. The word defeat appears in all the seven phrases, but the word tenacious is not directly quoted in any of them.

A deeper analysis can lead the reader to observe the following indirectly mentioned in all of them. This author is talking about tenacity. How is tenacity related to defeat? If somebody is attempting to reach a goal, and he/she is defeated. How come can this person overcome defeat? The only way to do so is to be tenacious, able to stand up after a fall, to inspire the human being to recover because his/her sense of purpose has not been achieved. Procrastination may interfere with their iron will with the justification of a failure. If a person is not tenacious, most likely he/she will give up repeating the failed undertaking and the defeat of his sense of purpose might confuse them. Having said so, if the individual is tenacious, he will not accept defeat, stand up, go back to analyze what went wrong and to insist on succeeding maybe trying different ways.

From my book *May Empathy Lead to Sense of Purpose through Tenacity*, I am copying the three definitions:

"The term "**empathy**" is used to describe a wide range of experiences. Emotion researchers generally **define empathy** as the ability to sense other people's emotions, coupled with the ability to imagine what someone else might be thinking or feeling.

Empathy is the capacity to understand or feel what another person is experiencing from within their frame of reference, that is, the capacity to place oneself in another's position."

"**Sense of Purpose** (or meaning) is the motivation that drives a human being toward a satisfying future. It also helps that person to get the most from the things he/she does and achieves –– in an either large or small way –– right on the spot.

When people have a **sense of purpose**, they tend to have increased optimism, resiliency, and hope. Experiencing joy, happiness, and satisfaction more often, sense of purpose leads to better physical and mental health."

"**Tenacity** is defined as being able to grip something firmly, determined, tenaciously and consistently. If someone is called tenacious, he/she probably is the kind of person who never gives up and never stops trying, someone who does whatever is required to accomplish a goal. That person can also be categorized as stubborn. Tenacity is maintaining forward momentum going with a game plan, a strategy, and the determination to keep dreams alive even in the face of seemingly insurmountable odds. Tenacity is an antonym for weakness. Tenacious is about steadily moving forward."

Establishing one possible sequence among the three words, I will start with sense of purpose. When somebody starts to pursue an objective, most likely it will be in connection to his sense of purpose. For example, when I was trying to write my first dissertation, I was basing my work on my experience in solving economic problems involving the use of mathematics. Therefore, my sense of purpose was to become doctor in economic science. I was supposed to suffer opposition from colleagues who had so far not being able to solve a complex mathematically economic issue. I previously had several publications, gotten the experience of receiving good and not so good comments, from which I found alternative ways to prove the validity of my mathematical models.

From my book *Havana-Merida-Chicago (A Journey to Freedom)*, during the difficult process of receiving several criticisms I was able to be in my opponents' shoes, and be prepared to face simple, complex, and difficult opposition. I understood my 'temporary enemies' frustration and intention to stop my scientific career, or at least to delay the process. I also counted on my wife's support. Therefore, my first pre-defense was rejected, but I was not defeated and decided to write a second version. Additionally, I looked for some help from a prestigious Soviet PhD, who was kind enough to grant me five scientific sessions, in which I translated my dissertation from Spanish to Russian. After. the final session was over, I asked him whether my work had a solid scientific basis. His answer not only was affirmative, but also, he offered himself to be present in the second pre-defense of my dissertation. Dr. Sytnik also brought another colleague to participate in the meeting, and the second version of the dissertation was almost unanimously accepted. Therefore, I now counted on the Soviet empathetic representatives. My Cuban peers were convinced that my work had a solid scientific basis. At the end of the day everybody appeared to be satisfied.

I still had to face more obstacles, like passing four exams (philosophy, foreign language, mathematical, and economics). I passed the first three with flying colors, but the exam of economics couldn't be held in Cuba, because there were not enough members of the special committee appointed to deal with economic problems.

So, I asked Dr. Sytnik when he was supposed to return to Kiev. His answer was in one month. Apparently, I wouldn't have been able to finish it in Havana. Two months later, the President of Havana University received an invitation from the President of the University of Kiev inviting professor Antonio Morales-Pita him for a nine months stay to finish his PhD. I left Havana in September 1981, and through two additional pre-defenses plus an exam of Political Economy, on May 20, 1982, I became PhD in Mathematical Economics.

Therefore, the stages of sense of purpose and empathy were strengthened by my solid tenacity. I was ready to become PhD going through the thick and thin.

If the readers revise each one of the seven famous phrases related to overcoming battles, it would be clear to them that without tenacity, it would have been impossible to beat or to overcome defeat.

Which would be necessary steps to be in control of your health?

This author proposes the following steps in this interesting world of living healthily:

1. To learn about the possible health issues, and how to deal with them.
2. To know what grade of participation is requested from the medical doctors, the physical therapists, and patients.
3. To know the role of exercises and losing weight according to physical therapists' and medical doctors' opinions, recommendations, and instructions.
4. The patients should be aware of their physical and mental participation in the exercises.
5. To be aware of the patients' determinations to continue exercising and keeping a stable weight in a permanent way, despite any sicknesses which might suddenly appear.
6. To include happiness and self-satisfaction in the exercises.
7. To recognize the benefits of both exercising and losing weight, for everybody, but especially for seniors, who are the most needing human beings to require staying healthy.
8. To be aware and to celebrate small victories against procrastination, which may appear as temporary inconveniences, apparent defeats, or discouragements.
9. **It is very important to exercise systematically, regardless of your mood. It is highly recommended to do your best**

to keep the enthusiasm, to feel the improvement in the strength of the muscles, in achieving small victories.

10. To be mindful about the progresses as time goes by. It is important to be aware of, conscious, acquainted with, and watchful of as soon as the first manifestation of tiredness, reluctance, or discouragement pops up. Impose your iron will, inspire yourself to keep going despite temporary emotional or mental discouragements.

11. Say no to negative feelings. Enjoy your successes.

12. Prepare yourself conscientiously to get over a possible fall. Don't' get discouraged if it happens because of an unexpected obstacle, barrier, or impediment. If the problems refer to your health, rush to the emergency room and put yourself in the medical doctors' hands.

13. Feel the internal happiness of continuing demanding more effort from your muscles and your brain, and reward yourself whenever the slightest victory appears.

14. If losses of memory appear in your life. Don't get discouraged. Try to sleep at least 7 hours to keep your brain rested.

15. Try to be optimistic regardless of possible recoils or drawbacks.

16. If the reader loves to sing, he/she should do it very often, regardless of having a rooster when singing. According to my pulmonologist, to sing is good for your lungs.

What to do if health is not doing well?

a) Fever To experience high temperatures, the medical community generally defines a fever as a body temperature above 100.4 degrees Fahrenheit. A body temp **between 100.4 and 102.2 degree** is usually considered a low-grade fever. https (//www.osfhealthcare.org). **Consider seeing a doctor if: a).** Fever lasts longer than three to five days; b) Fever doesn't respond to fever-reducing medications, such as acetaminophen or ibuprofen (Tylenol or Advil); c) Other symptoms include confusion, neck stiffness or sensitivity to light.

b) To experience lack of sleep for several days, to lose appetite, to feel unwilling to do simple tasks.
c) To feel cold and unwilling to go out.
d) To feel pain for more than 24 hours.
e) To be sad for unknown justifiable reasons.
f) To lose energy to realize small tasks,
g) To feel sad for unknown reasons.
h) To feel reluctant to undertake jobs normally realized with little effort.

I am a generally enthusiastic man, able to undertake simultaneously sometimes more than one occupation. I love to exercise; therefore, I normally do it every day regardless how good or bad day I am going through.

Under normal circumstances, I start exercising in the early morning after taking my morning medicines. They are exercises I have learned from previous PT sessions with three specialists. Exercise "A" I normally need half-an-hour. After that – every other day – I exercise for my muscles, legs, arms in the elliptical and the stationary bike for one hour. Exercise "B" walking with my cane on the floor. Exercise "C" walking at least 1.5 miles in one hour. My daily average since the last two weeks is 2.5 miles (1.2 hours every day). In terms of minutes per week:

Exercise "A" : 30 minutes X 7 days	=	210 minutes / week
Exercise "B": 60 minutes X 3 hours	=	180"
Exercise "C" 80 minutes X 7 days	=	560 "
Total minutes per week	=	950"

I have adopted this system for two weeks now, and the results are astounding because I can walk at a normal pace (never running) with my cane in the air without being neither tired, or feeling pain in my legs, waist, feet, or arms. I introduce walking through different streets, sometimes even singing to get entertained. I can enjoy exercising because the good results are obvious. I try to introduce small variations to make exercising more enjoyable, never boring.

I am almost 82 years old, but feel happy, optimistic, busy writing manuscripts, promoting sales, exercising, going to church every Sunday, as a true house husband, after my wife died in 2015, and… traveling around the world. If to be old means to lose energy, to be sad, to be lazy without knowing what to do, then I am not mentally old. Since I was a professor for fifty-four years and retired at seventy-six, I enjoy life and keep doing my legacy "teaching through my books". Therefore, I will continue teaching after death through my books. It is wonderful to feel that my teaching will survive me. Whenever someone reads any of my books, and feels inspired to go ahead in life, regardless of whether I am alive, I will continue teaching. Thanks be to God!

As far as I know, this is a book that, besides briefly entering into types of exercises, which have been recommended by outstanding writers, is the first one to deal with, and to emphasize, the importance of adding systematic exercising after finishing the sessions with the specialist in physical therapy.

My point is that all the previously consulted books, introduce quite a number of exercises, but do not mention the need to be tenacious in order to change their lives forever. To exercise is the duty of every patient, which is exclusively in their hands. It is not possible for writers in following up with the results of learning from their books. They cannot follow up with the patients. This book emphasizes – for the first time – the imminent need to continue exercising forever. This responsibility is theirs, not of the authors of the exercises.

I inherited passion for exercising from my mother, who – being illiterate – never stopped exercising during her 88 years of age, spreading the word among, and demanding her children to follow her example. I was the last child of the couple and – since I was born – I could see and get enthusiastic to have a slender mother, who died due to a mistake during a Christmas party at home, at 88 years old. My siblings also inherited her gens, but, unfortunately, were not passionate about exercising.

My mother followed closely my scientific development. Under certain occasions, whenever I complained to her that it was hard for me to accomplish any undertaking, she always "shocked me up" insisting that I didn't have any right to give in, and that I should encourage myself with her example (when I was born, she was illiterate at 31, and she finished high school at 75). She was even scolding me for having felt weaker than my obstacles. When I was in my last stage of my second doctorate, just one week before the defense of my dissertation, she managed to go to Kiev – which is extremely difficult for a Cuban - with my youngest sister as a tourist. My mother participated in every activity and was an example for all the tourists, who were younger than she.

It may be interesting if I write in table whatever a certain process of overcoming procrastination in exercising:

First session of exercises per week

1. If possible, write a diary or in whatever piece of paper the exercising activities planned for the week.
2. Write a check mark in the process of exercising, evaluating as A,B,C or D your results. You would be your own evaluator.
3. Every week, find the average # of exercises, or minutes required to exercise.
4. If the average of every week in minutes is increasing, congratulate yourself in whatever healthy way you can.

Repeat the exercises for the four weeks of the month, and do a self-evaluation..

It would be wonderful if you are able to build a succession of weeks in a month, and compare it with the preceding one.

It is very important that you create your own goals, and evaluate them.

I show my primary care physician the results whenever I attend his office. He, himself, is suggesting or instructing me. For example, he asked me if I was able to stand up after being seated. I did it right away. But I added the exercise to the rest of them, and could see that I was little by little adding more repetitions. One month later, I added to stand up from the mattress I exercise with, and I COULD. In the following week, I was adding two repetitions from the floor.

It is interesting to be your own physical therapist. You can create something different and add interest to the exercises. To become the owner of your training may improve your self-esteem. After receiving sessions of exercises from a PT, then one has two options: 1. To continue exercising, getting stronger, and strengthening your body beyond your expectations. 2. To stop exercising (maybe fewer days per week, or fewer minutes per day, and as a result one can simply stop exercising) . You can take it for granted that within some months, you will return once again to the PT because your pain and problems came back. As a consequence, you will have to spend money twice, despite the fact that you could have avoided the second session if you have continued exercising. So, this problem is a healthy issue, combined with an economic one. You are the responsible for getting cured or getting a second round because you couldn't stick to the exercises. No physical trainer is able to cure you, if you don't take in your hands the possibility of being cured, and getting much more stronger than you were at the beginning of the process.

Food for thought

1. If the reader is a senior, would reading this chapter motivate him/her to introduce exercising into their lives?
2. What about if this question is asked to a middle-aged person who is not yet accustomed to exercising?
3. Generally addressing to all readers of this book, would they feel ready to start exercising on a regular basis with or without requiring walking dogs?

CHAPTER VII

Is There a Relationship between Systematic Exercising and Tenacity and Sense of Purpose?

<u>Famous phrases about exercising</u>

"The reason I exercise is for the quality of life I enjoy."
Kenneth H. Cooper

"The only bad workout is the one that didn't happen."
Anonymous

"Exercise is a celebration of what your body can do. Not a punishment for what you h<u>ate</u>."
Anonymous

. "Daily exercise is one of the keys to excellent health."
ATGW **Anti - Tank Guided Weapon**

"For me, exercise is more than just physical – it's therapeutic."
Anonymous

. "Once you <u>see</u> results, it becomes an addiction."
Anonymous

. "You have to exercise, or at some point you'll just break down."
Barack Obama

"When it comes to health and well-being, regular exercise is about as close to a magic potion as you can get."
Tich Nhat Hanh

W HAT IS THE opinion of the World Health Organization? https://www.who.int/health-topics/physical-activity

Overview

"Regular physical activity is proven to help prevent and manage noncommunicable diseases (NCDs) such as heart disease, stroke, diabetes, and several cancers. It also helps prevent hypertension, maintain healthy body weight, and can improve mental health, quality of life and well-being.

Physical activity refers to all movements. Popular ways to be active include walking, cycling, wheeling, sports, active recreation, and play, and can be done at any level of skill and for enjoyment by everybody.

Yet, current global estimates show one in four adults and eighty-one % of adolescents do not do enough physical activity. Furthermore, as countries develop economically, levels of inactivity increase and can be as high as seventy %, due to changing transport patterns, increased use of technology for work and recreation, cultural values and increasing sedentary behaviors.

Increased levels of physical inactivity have negative impacts on health systems, the environment, economic development, community well-being and quality of life.

The **WHO Global action plan on physical activity 2018–2030: more active people for a healthier world,** provides a framework of effective and feasible policy actions which can help support, retain and increase physical activity through cross-government and multisectoral partnerships across all settings, as a coordinated and comprehensive response".

Impact

"Physical inactivity is one of the leading risk factors for noncommunicable diseases (NCDs) and death worldwide. It increases the risk of cancer, heart disease, stroke, and diabetes by 20–30%. It is estimated that four to five million deaths per year could be averted if the global population was more active.

One in four adults – and four out of five adolescents don't do enough physical activity. Women and girls generally are less active than men and boys, widening health inequalities. Older adults and people living with disabilities are also less likely to be active and miss out on the physical, mental, and social health benefits.

Physical inactivity burdens society through the hidden and growing cost of medical care and loss of productivity. Estimates from 2016 show that physical inactivity cost the health system US$ 54 billion and resulted in US$ 14 billion in economic losses. Estimates from both high-income, as well as low- and middle-income countries (LMICs) indicate that between 1–3% of national health care expenditures are attributable to physical inactivity.

If regular physical activity is so vital for achieving, keeping, improving health, and reducing falls, why the number of exercising seniors is either stagnating or descending.

According to this author's experience based on his systematic participation in physical exercising for almost 25 years after his heart attack in 1998, the main obstacle that seniors need to win a victory over is their <u>lack of tenacity</u>. There are certain excuses to justify their lack of passion for physical exercise; namely, tiredness, and getting older. I highly recommend the readers to enter in www.bing.com, where they will find ten excuses for not to exercise; namely: I am too tired, I don't have time, my kids are at home, gym memberships are too expensive, no one will exercise with me, I hate to sweat, It's not fun, I'm embarrassed by how I look, the skinny people will laugh at me, I don't have any workout cloth. I highly recommend an antidote, to meditate and to act against procrastination, to postpone actions for another day.

Not always I am in the mood for exercising, but I am a tenacious man, and say to myself: "Common, don't hesitate, think about improvement to be achieved in your health. The reward in health may delay, but the harder you exercise, the sooner they will be part of your healthy habits."

<u>Famous phrases about tenacity</u>

If I have anything, it's tenacity."
Hal Sparks

"It's hard to beat a person who never gives up.
Anonymous

"My strength lies solely in my tenacity."
Louis Pasteur

"If you fell down yesterday, stand up today."
H.G. Wells

"Tenacity is the mother of progress."
Valerie M. Hudson

"Tenacity isn't just the most important thing,
It's the only thing." Mavin Leno

Albert Einstein famously said that there was nothing so remarkable about him except for his curiosity, which is another word for tenacity: The man stayed up for days at a time solving his mind-bending equations. Nothing could stop him. Ditto for Edison -- his thousands of failed experiments before lighting the first bulb is the definition of tenacity. Fast-forward to modern times and we have JK Rowling, who was rejected by at least a dozen publishers before *Harry Potter* became a bestseller.

Tenacity is the thread that binds all innovators, entrepreneurs, and problem solvers to one another. And if you want to join their ranks, this is the one eight-letter trait you've simply got to master. Here's how the most successful entrepreneurs do it.

Some of Albert Einstein's – listed below - famous phrases are related to different ways to materialize tenacity, even though the word was not mentioned in any of the phrases. His intelligence allowed him to express how tenacity is achieved, as well as how it is identified.

Here there are some of his most famous phrases

"If you want to live a happy life, tie it to a
goal, not to people or things." --

"A person who has never made a mistake
has never tried anything new." -

"We cannot solve our problems with the same
thinking we used when we created them"

"Learn from yesterday, live for today, hope for tomorrow.
The important thing is not to stop questioning."

"The leader is one who, out of the clutter, brings simplicity...
Out of discord, harmony... And out of difficulty, opportunity."

"The value of achievement lies in the achieving."

You have to learn the rules of the game, and then, you have to play it better than anyone else."

"Know where to find the information and how to use it. That's the secret of success."

Definition of the word tenacity

From page xiii of my book May Empathy Lead to Sense of Purpose through I Tenacity? I am copying my own definition of tenacity:

"Tenacity

Browsing definitions of tenacity in Google and Wikipedia, this author has concluded that: **Tenacity** is defined as being able to grip something firmly grip, determined, tenaciously and consistently. If someone is called tenacious, he/she probably is the kind of person who never gives up and never stops trying, someone who does whatever is required to accomplish a goal. That person can also be categorized as stubborn. Tenacity is maintaining forward momentum going with a game plan, a strategy, and the determination to keep dreams alive even in the face of seemingly insurmountable odds. Tenacity is an antonym for weakness. Tenacious is about steadily moving forward. The difference between perseverance and tenacity is that perseverance is continuing in a course of action without regard to discouragement, opposition or previous failures, while tenacity is the quality of staying as being tenacious and successful most likely by having attempted to solve the problem in different ways."

What makes a person tenacious?

Tenacious persons are very determined –and not willing to

stop –when they are trying to achieve something. They are determined and ambitious.

What adjectives can be applied to a tenacious person; for example, persistent; stubborn, courageous, holding firmly to a tenacious grip and having a retentive memory, unwilling to yield or give up besides having good memory.

Which are the components of a tenacious person. He or she is very determined and is not willing to stop when trying to achieve something. In a tenacious person his/her tenacious <u>ideas</u>, <u>beliefs</u>, or <u>habits</u> <u>continue</u> for a long time and are difficult to change; not easily pulled apart ; cohesive; tending to adhere or cling especially to another substance; persistent in maintaining, adhering to, or seeking something valued or desired; retentive.

If tenacious persons start exercising and feel improvement in their health, (according to this author's opinion) there is a probability that they will continue this activity for a long time.

Tenacious people are more likely to succeed in whatever activity they are specialized.

In general terms, it is very hard to deduct conclusions about tenacity because of lack of data, but I do have a firsthand information about my family.

Personal analysis of my family: my mother, my father, myself, my wife. The first three persons were fundamentally tenacious. My mother (being illiterate) was able to foster in her four children love for punctual attending and studying primary school. My mother was always active spreading enthusiasm and hard work all around her. My father didn't allow her to work outside home. When he died; she started to work outside home, but, from her first job in a children's cloth factory, she won a prize for being number one, breaking all norms at 65 years old; she was an active member of the Cuban Women association. She was tireless. She was illiterate until completing 51 years (because her original family was very poor) and finished high school at 80 years old. She was always an example for the different study groups she was part of.

My father systematically worked as stevedore at the main market in Havana for almost 50 years, he did not have vacations and was never absent, including during hurricanes attacking Havana.

I was the ....last children of the couple, the first member of the family to finish a bachelor's degree, to become an instructor starting in his third year of bachelorship, teaching students for two years before graduating, finishing a Master's degree in Operational Research in Glasgow, Scotland, his first and second PhD in the former Soviet Union, becoming a professor for 54 years at the University of Havana, the Merida Institute of Technology in Mexico, and 22 years at DePaul University, writer of 12 books, inspirational speaker promoting his books, and polyglot in Spanish, English, Russian, Italian and French.

My wife was an extraordinary university student, teacher, in Mexican universities and at St. Augustine College in Chicago. When she arrived at the US with me from Cuba, she did not know English, she learned it during three years to the point of becoming a teacher of Business in Spanish and English at St. Augustine College. She could not be tenacious in two directions: smoking and exercising. Her most outstanding merit was to transform the man in her life from being a selfish lady's man to becoming an empathetic and loyal husband during their forty years, six months and one day of incredible togetherness. She had to be deeply in love with Antonio, overcoming difficulties with his husband's mother, children, first wife, homeless and the Cuban government. Her one-of-a-kind attitude was contained in my eighth book *Gladys, My Unforgettable Love*.

In all the tenacious members of my family were present stubbornness, firmly gripped tenacity, retentiveness, unwillingness to yield or give up, adhesiveness, cohesiveness, deep determination of ending what was initiated.

In terms of percentages 4 people out of 20 including some members of my wife's family, were generally tenacious, therefore, make 25%.

As a professor in Cuba, Mexico, and the United States, I taught approximately 10,000 students. If I take the number of students receiving "A" evaluations their final grades during more than five decades, it would be hard to have more than 20% outstanding students. –

Although, from a statistical perspective, it is extremely difficult – during my fifty-four year career - to calculate or estimate the percentage of outstanding students. From an empirical standpoint– under the assumption that excellent students were more likely to be tenacious because they attended to most of my classes, and were attentive, and actively participating in the classes– I would estimate that somewhere between 10 to 20% of my students had chances of being tenacious.

Unfortunately, as far as this writer knows, there do not exist data correlating exercising and tenacity.

Is It possible to introduce tenacity into your habits in a sustainable way? Yes, if you are convinced and decided to prioritize being healthier. The process will not be easy, but it is worth-while to do the effort. Just compare starting to exercise with a sound investment. At the beginning, there is a process of learning, assimilating, analyzing results. As you get used to keep active, little by little you can identify yourself with the result, when you feel stronger, and happier, you will be going in the right direction.

I highly recommend my readers to: a) add happiness; b) start in an optimistic mood; c) to start with a smile on your face; d) try hard to defeat postponements; e) to eliminate excuses of attempting another day. In other words, try hard and persistently to defeat the ghost of procrastination.

Tenacity and procrastination are opposite poles. If an individual is tenacious, he/she will be ready to act immediately; or, as soon as possible, in the process of starting exercising. If the individual is a procrastinator, he/she will never force himself to exercise.

This author came across the paper "EXP: Tenacity: Self-Regulation of Attention and Its Relationship with Learning" by Constance Steinkuehler, Kurt Squire, and Richard Davidson from the University of Wisconsin-Madison. It proposes a different way of defining tenacity as a self-regulation. They define the factors, grit, tenacity, and perseverance as non-cognitive factors. I totally agree with the following two sentences in the paper, which I am copying herein: "Self-regulation skills are critical for success in today's era of rapid technological and social change. Luckily, evidence is accumulating that such skills can be taught."

Which are the cognitive skills? According to Google, they are eight skills, in this classification: attention, memory; self-awareness, reasoning, motivation and goal setting, association capacity, cognitive flexibility, and problem-solving.

What is meant by problem solving according to Oxford language? *It is the process of finding solutions to difficult or complex issues.*

Learning from mistakes (**self-regulation**) was a significant predictor of coping and confidence, **tenacity** was related to adaptation, and tolerance to not **cognitive factors**, not related to the process of acquiring knowledge through the senses, experience, or reasoning such as grit+tenacity+ perseverance.

Why do this author believe that it is necessary to include a sort of bridge between tenacity and systematic exercising? It seems to this author that between systematic exercising and tenacity, an important word is missing, that is to say, sense of purpose. Therefore, what is sense of purpose?

☐ From page xii of my same previously mentioned book:

"**Sense of Purpose** (or meaning) is the motivation that drives a human being toward a satisfying future. It also helps that person to get the most from the things he/she does and achieves –– in an either large or small way –– right on the spot.

When people have a **sense of purpose**, they tend to have increased optimism, resiliency, and hope. Experiencing joy, happiness, and satisfaction more often leads to better physical and mental health.

Why Having a Sense of Purpose is Important?

The dictionary defines "purpose" as the reason for which something exists or is done, made or used. Sounds boring, huh? But when you break it down, it turns out that purpose is important––to your physical, mental, and emotional health. It's that big.

So, what is the readers' purpose? According to researcher

William Damon, who wrote *A Path to Purpose*, it is "a stable and generalized intention to accomplish something that is at the same time meaningful to the self and consequential for the world beyond the self."

In fact, that meaningful intention can help people to stay focused on the things that matter most to them like family, friends, faith, career and more. It helps them to prioritize their lives —allowing them to walk away from certain people or activities that don't serve their purpose. It's a main driver to stay motivated when things get tough, so they can set and meet short and long-term goals. And maybe most of all, it makes them feel like making a difference in the world."

Why is the phrase "sense of purpose" intermediate between exercising and tenacity?.

I asked the readers to attempt answering the following question:

Does the word "exercising" necessarily implies that it is systematic? Or could it be true for one or two weeks (for example, as part of a treatment with a physical trainer)?. Exercising is an indispensable means of getting stronger, which consequently may help avoid falls especially for seniors, whose muscles and bones are not so strong as they were in their young and medium-age years.

Therefore, ..

Citing some examples of having tenacity following my sense of purpose deeply rooted attitude.

Pages 45 to 47 of **Havana-Merida-Chicago (A Journey to Freedom)**

My second PhD: "Development and Optimal Planning of the Industrial -Agricultural Sugar Complex in Cuba" took me eight years of intense research.

"The leaders of the ministers of Higher Education and Sugar agreed with my method of planning the initial and final period of harvesting cane. They helped me grow as a research leader and to write the chapters of my doctoral dissertation. In the period of 1985–1990, I visited Kiev on three occasions to prepare myself for the big doctoral dissertation. It took me at least five years to persuade these ministers about the convenience of introducing my mathematical models into the planning system of the Minister of Sugar. I had to overcome several administrative obstacles, but at the end I could finish this preliminary stage of my research.

A big new problem appeared in the horizon at the end of this period. The relations between the former Soviet Union (then in the"perestroika" process) and Cuba were no longer friendly. The number of persons in candidacies was reduced considerably, and that of doctoral candidates decidedly diminished, especially in social sciences.

So, during the last few years of the eighties, to make the long story short, the main difficulties were as follows: (a) I had to obtain the rubles in Cuba because the Soviet party no longer paid Cubans' expenses; (b) a special permit was required from the Cuban Communist Party to travel to the Soviet Union to pursue a scientific degree in social sciences; (c) the Soviet institutions were not ready to arrange for visiting candidates' lodging, which had to be solved by the Cuban office of the Ministry of Higher Education in Moscow; (d) the Soviet system was having political and societal difficulties, and helping Cubans was no longer a priority; (e) the mail between Havana and any Soviet city was difficult, so it was necessary to find somebody going specifically to Kiev to carry versions of the dissertation to be revised, and then bring them back to Cuba.

Firmly believing in myself, standing up after temporary falling, In 1989, I could solve all the previous inconveniences, but just one week before leaving Cuba, the Politburo of the Cuban Communist Party issued an order that no Cuban professor was allowed to go to the Soviet Union to finish any degree in social science. Everything halted. My tenacity couldn't allow me to give up. So, what did I do?

My only option would be to defend the dissertation in Cuba, but again after months of searching for members of the doctoral committee, the impossibility of creating a Cuban committee of doctors in economics was evident. In Cuba there were only two doctors in economics, and five doctors were required. Even though I had finished my doctoral dissertation written in Russian, all I could do was to wait.

I didn't give up. I had gone through tenebrous and gloomy periods, and I fervently wanted to hold my second PhD. Unexpectedly, in February 1990, I was informed that my case had been approved to go to Kiev, since I was the only candidate, who had already concluded his second dissertation.

On February 28, 1990, one of my friends in Kiev had arranged my lodging at a modest rate, and I had 1,200 rubles- handed to me by the Minister of High Education in Cuba - to be spent during the six months needed to finish the work. I was -then- in the last stage of achieving my second doctoral degree.

The period of March–September 1990, residing in Kiev, was full of difficulties. Cubans were not welcomed any longer in Kiev. The same typist who did my candidate dissertation for 100 rubles in 1982 was now asking for US dollars, and I had to type my own dissertation in Russian. Paper was very scarce in Kiev, and I had to rely on all my friends to get it. The news about the Chernobyl nuclear explosion was widely known. I learned that by staying in Kiev my health was seriously threatened. Finally, the food was scarce and even more expensive than it had been in the previous years.

At last, on September 19, 1990, I defended my second doctoral dissertation, which contained much of my work during the period of 1982 – 1989 on the academic and research team, more than 40 papers and presentations, and three books. Because I did not know whether or when the Soviet Union would collapse, I kept copies of all of the documents of my defense, the opponents' opinions, and especially the conclusions of the committee to grant me the degree. Shortly after returning to Cuba, I learned that the Soviet Union had collapsed and that most likely the National Soviet Committee for Granting Scientific Degrees had been dissolved. I did not know whether someday I would ever have my diploma. I had reached the highest scientific degree and was the only professor at the University of Havana having that degree, whereby I expected to be able to apply my knowledge to help the economy of Cuba."

As I had always done whenever I tried to accomplish a goal, I had the peace of mind of having done everything possible to achieve the degree. Therefore, I was in peace of mind with myself.

I had so far not written which was my sense of purpose. As a professor, scholar, Cuban born scientist, **I needed to hold my second doctoral decree.** Making the summary short, a) I was chosen as professor of Operational Research being a nongraduate student of Marxist Economics; b) I was the only faculty, which required only ten years to become professor; c) the first Cuban professor to hold a Master's degree, at the University of Strathclyde in Glasgow, Scotland; d) the first professor to hold doctorate at the Faculty of Economics in 1982; e) the only professor to hold a second doctorate in Economics, in 1990; f) the only professor to be included in an exterchange of professors between the University of Havana and the University of Chicago in 1994; g) the only professor speaking five languages; h) the only Cuban economics-professor awarded the Excellence in Teaching Award at DePaul University in 2007; i) during fifty four years I worked as a professor and scholar, and retired in 2016 having instructed at least 10,000 Cuban, Mexican and American students. Consequently, my sense of purpose was to finish my second doctoral decree. I didn't know, but I needed to receive the diploma representing the end of my educational career as a scholar.

Therefore, to be a successful educator was in my soul since I became adult. I had to face innumerable challenges, defeats, and successes, but – whenever I fell – right away l stood up. I had to be profoundly tenacious to materialize my sense of purpose. At the end of the day, by still unknown reasons, I successfully received my doctoral document four years after I defended it.

My mother's sense or purpose was to study hard, to learn, to exercise so exercise systematically, and to be an example for her family, friends and human beings appearing in her life. She was an example of a hardworker everywhere she was present, at home, at primary school after turning 51 years old, during vacation times, even in a trip from Havana to the Soviet Union close to turning 80 years old, while I was finishing my second doctorate in Kiev. Although she was illiterate because she was born in a very poor family that could not afford her studies because she had to wash clothes to help her eleven siblings. She never said "no" to herself, to help people in need, to become an example wherever she was present. She was totally tenacious in exercising systematically on a bike made of wood at home and running along the house for all her life. She tried to infuse tenacity in all her children, but not all of them continued her example after getting married. Although she experienced defeats, she always stood up right away. I never saw my mother sad, defeated, discouraged. Her sense of purpose was to be useful to her family, to her friends, and to everybody sharing his/her life with her. She loved education and was able to go from first grade at her early fifties to high school graduate close to her eighties.

My mother never accepted failures from me. Whenever I was defeated in any of my goals, she immediately demanded me to stand up, never to say that I hadn't be able to achieve.

The triumphal combination of exercising, tenacity, and sense of purpose plus resilience

After relating the previous three words to the author's life, is it possible and convenient for seniors to incorporate them into their lives?

My answer is yes. From lexico.com this author found the following phrase: "Through an incorporate resilience slighted confidence restores itself"

The definition of resilience, from Merrian Webster, is the following " resilience means an ability to recover from or adjust easily to misfortune or change."

Being a eighty-two years old senior, through my empathetic trait, my live experience meeting seniors in Cuba, Scotland, Mexico, the former Soviet Union, the United States, and my travel trips around the world, I can be in the shoes of optimistic, pessimistic, realistic, pragmatic, and idealistic seniors.

<u>Let's start with optimistic seniors</u>. Their ages are in the range of seventy to eighty years old, have so far never fallen, and learned that the combination of exercising, tenacity, sense of purpose and resilience can help them avoiding a fall.

First step: have they materialized their senses of purpose? Do they feel satisfied with their achievements in their main goals?

Second step: do they exercise systematically at least every other day?

Third step: are they generally tenacious in pursuing their main goals, standing up after a fall, and trying not to postpone for tomorrow what is due to be done today?

Fourth step: are they resilient enough to withstand or recover quickly from difficult conditions especially in the continuation of exercising as a goal in their lives?

Chances are that seniors answering "yes "to the four questions will be healthy and ready not to fall in the process of getting older. My two parents, and siblings––as far as I know and remember –– never fell regardless of their old ages. I experienced one fall last year and went to the Emergency Room of Northwestern Hospital for two days. They discovered that the reason for the fall was the increased dosage of a prescription for controlling my blood pressure, but my brain was in a very good shape.

My personal situation is: a) my sense of purpose is to continue teaching through my books, whose main purpose is to continue teaching and helping humanity; b) I have been exercising systematically since September 1998 when I had a heart attack, and learned about the importance of physical exercising and reducing weight; c) I definitely am a tenacious main; d) whenever I have not succeeded in meeting any of my goals, I am resilient enough to "stand up" and to start all over again with determination.

Some of my slogans are NEVER TO SAY "NO" to myself. "to keep on trying", "never to give up " "feeling to have done all I could". If I ever fall again, for an unexpected circumstance, I would have the peace of mind of knowing that I did all I could to avoid it.

Let's concentrate our attention in the extreme case of pessimistic seniors

Going through the same four steps as I did in the case of optimistic seniors, chances are that they had not been basically successful materializing their senses of purpose, or had not been physical systematically exercising during decades, neither conversely tenacious in whatever goal they have self-assigned, or especially following recommendations from physical therapists, and finally most of the times had not been resilient enough to recover their energy and continue defeating procrastination, which may suddenly appear when one is down for whatever reason.

Does this mean that there is no hope for pessimist seniors to avoid falling? Given my experience in conversation and working sessions for years with three excellent physical therapists, my answer is "no". If this type of seniors has lost their hope to get better and to avoid falling, this author believes that –– as long as there is life, and desire to live ––there is hope to improve. They may be treated by psychologists and medical doctors who can help them to recover trust in themselves.

My personal recommendation to this type of seniors is to ask for their help. If a pessimistic individual feels the need and the will to stop this negative trait and lacks exercising, tenacity, sense of purpose and resilience, this author recommends the pessimistic seniors to see in which one of the four the following procedure is easier for them to start with: exercising, tenacity, sense of purpose or resilience.

This author recommends to start with sense of purpose, which facilitates building tenacity may start, and resilience, and "opens the door" to exercising as a means of feeling better, adding fun to life, allowing a better control of your help.

This author has found a new word "ikigai", which is a Japanese concept referring to something that gives a person a sense of purpose. Ikigai brings meaning, purpose,and fulfillment to your life,while also contributes to the goods of others. Ikigai is the intersection of passion, talent, and potential to benefit others

What are the 10 rules of ikigai? According to www.indiatoday. in the ten rules of Ikigai by Hector Garcia and Francesc Miralles include: "**Stay active. Don't retire; Take it slow; Get in shape; Live in the moment; Reconnect with nature; Smile; Surround yourself with good friends; Give thanks; and Follow your Ikigai**".

Can an individual build the skill of tenacity? According to Google, and my own personal experience. Tenacity my start **by making up your mind to win and be a winner**! Keep moving toward what you want. Don't give up on your dreams, and don't give in to quitting. Hold on to what you believe.

Tenacity is also defined as "persistent determination". **It is considered a good character trait** since tenacious characters will achieve a goal they set despite any difficulties encountered in the way.

Sometimes one receives an unexpected reverse or setback to awaken your love for life, desire for enjoying life, and to develop tenacity. When I had an unexpected heart attack when I was only 58 years old, I was shown a series of videos showing the reasons for that unfortunate event. I, then, learned the positive effect of eating fruits and vegetables, to reduce consumption of salt, fats, beef, bacon, ham, and to include and to increase fish, skinless chicken, and turkey. To reduce my weight in a slow but systematic way and to start physical exercises in a systematic way. To be shown blocked arteries around the heart was also a solid way of being aware of the consequences of unhealthy eating habits. For me, it was indispensable saving my life through systematic exercises.

This author has created additional fun to exercises by: enjoying exercising, realizing how the strength of my muscles is improving, how I am feeling in control on my health, including variations in the activity, choosing a relative constant time for exercising just after waking up, the frequent increase in the number of times I exercise, including singing, and adding a one-mile walk every day, which I am detailing in the following paragraph.

The iphone automatically registers data during the last six weeks:

a) from 3,441 to 7,506 steps; b) my initial goal was one mile per day. During the week from August 7 to 13 has been from 1.5 to 3, with an average of 2.4 miles per day.

Before adopting this daily goal, I could walk five blocks without any pain, but resting one minute in the middle of the distance; since the last six weeks, I can walk ten, twelve, even twenty blocks without any pain or sign of tiredness. It is very encouraging to learn the improvement of my extra effort. I am also sleeping more hours. My brain wakes up ready to start a new day with a smile on my face. Since I am a singer, everyday I wake up singing.

A general advice to all seniors is to always check with your doctor before starting an exercise program. They can help you find activities that will increase your heart health without the risk of injury.

Food for thought

1. Have the readers in relation to exercising, started, continued for a time, and then stopped? If so, try to meditate which were the reasons for discontinuing.
2. Have some readers started a program of losing weight? How often did they check their numbers? Once they had lost pounds, had they came back to the original numbers? If so, did you recommence the process?
3. Have some readers felt their senses of purpose?

CHAPTER VIII

Can a dog help his/her owner to exercise?

"If your dog is fat, then you are not getting enough exercise"
Anonymous

"The term 'a dog is a man's best friend' was first used way back in 1789 by King Frederick of Prussia. He's claimed to say, "the only, absolute and best friend that a man has, in this selfish world, the only one that will not betray or deny him, is his Dog."
Google.com

THIS AUTHOR HAS never walked a dog. During his childhood and early youth he never saw anybody walking a dog at home. During his life living in Cuba, Mexico, Scotland, Ukraine, and the US, he never walked a dog. On certain occasions, in his early youth he was surprised by a dog's sudden sound barking that negatively shook him up. Another day I was ascending in the elevator of my building, and when the door opened, a huge dog was jumping and barking, and I complained to his owner. I have very good friends living outside Chicago who love their two dogs. Whenever I visited with them, I was on guard never close to the dogs, that were always jumping joyfully with their owners.

In conclusion I was never attracted to dogs. Just recently, after finishing my last session with a one-of-a-kind professional trainer and focusing on ways to incorporate tenacious exercising in human beings, I started to process information about the dogs' impact on their owners as far as walking is concerned. I concluded that walking the dogs requires their owners to exercise willingly or unwillingly, consciously, or unconsciously.

Talking to my trainers about my exceptional case of continuing exercising for years, they expected that only very few patients will continue their exercises just for a couple of weeks. But, in relation to the dogs, their owners for sure will need to walk them several times every day. Therefore, the dogs have the power to foster a sort of tenacity in their owners because —— regardless of the climatological conditions —— they would make it clear to their owners that they require to be walked.

Regardless of the owners' ages, the dogs demand their owners to walk them.

One of my best friends, Mr. Fadil Mehmedi,owner of Gill's Diner in Rockford, Illinois and in North Lake Cafe in North Lake, Texas, is a vivid example of a man, who is a very hard worker and loves dogs. I asked Fadil if he could write a note about his experience dealing with dogs as far as walking is concerned.

I am transcribing his contribution to this book:

"It is my opinion that dogs can play big role in the content of their owners' exercising activity as a means of avoiding falls.

Since 1988 I have been walking my dogs for the following purposes: a) to be accompanied by them; b) to stretch my legs in an interesting way; c) to exercise for about 45 minutes per day; d) to lose some weight in a consuetudinary way; e) I am a busy man owner of restaurants, and it has become hard for me to find time for exercising on my own; f) to reduce tension in my brain, feeling free from worries, just walking and sort of playing with them.

My dogs have become my daily emotional, physical, and recreational therapy.

From 2000 to 2022, I have been accepting dogs in my homes for several reasons: a) I love to play with them; and, therefore, temporarily reduce my stress coming from work and leading with different issues from my workers, my friends, and part of my family; b)I my personal case, it is my understanding that I have felt loyalty and dedication from my dogs to me, as well as from me to them?

Dogs are a safe way to protect my home from burglary.

I ask myself:

A) If I wouldn't have dogs at home, would I walk every night, or every day?

B) If either my wife or I hadn't had dogs at home, would we miss them?

C) Can you express in words how important are your dogs in relation to your psychological or physical health?

D) Dogs are very important and great part of my life as a family man, father, husband and business man .

E) Do I perceive a mental stress relief when bring around them whether I am at home, a park or anywhere else?"

My preferred priest, Father John Heschle, agreed to submit his special relation with dogs through an outstanding contribution

Pets can improve the quality of Human life, by Father John Heschle.

I grew up with animals wandering into our back yard from the woods. It was so exciting to see a family of dear, or even a possum in the yard. I grew up in a suburb just 15 miles west of NYC. Our home was never locked but was rife with dogs and puppies running all over the place. My Dad raised and bred Boxers. One or two of them even became Seeing Eye dogs for the blind. But puppies do relieve themselves as well as occasionally vomit in the most inconvenient places.

We always had dogs around our home, both pre breeds and 'waifs' we took in or adopted when they had no other home. When I was 13 I was blessed to get my own dog. A beautiful pure breed German Shepherd named Ginger. I had taken care of her all summer as the boy next door was home from College to work a construction job. He paid me to feed and walk her several times a day all summer. The dog and I fell in love and as September rolled around and he was going back to college, he asked me: "Would you like Ginger for your own dog? College Fraternity houses are no place for a 1 year old puppy. I will see her every time I'm home from College since you live next door."

At 13 I was overjoyed and tears came to my eyes to think I did not have to say good bye to Ginger. I had wondered how I'd cope missing her after being with her everyday all summer. Now she was mine. Yes, there is a God, I thought. She was devoted to me and I to her. She would be waiting for me when I got home after school or my part time job. We were inseparable. I still regret and remember the day I had to leave her with my sister to go off to complete my seminary training to become a priest.

Soon after I was sent to my first parish, Ginger died. I was grief stricken and heart broken. One day the Rectory door bell rang and there stood a woman from the next parish over with a 1 year old pure bred black Afghan puppy. Her name was Charm. The woman told me "Father, this dog was abandoned and needs a home. God pointed me to you. Will you take her?" By the time I could open my mouth, the woman was gone and I was holding the leash of the puppy. That day I fell in love with 'Sight Hounds' and since then I have had her, 3 Salukis, and now a Galgo rescued from Spain. Each dog had taught me how to love more deeply, fully and unconditionally- not because of how you look, your heritage, wealth, wisdom or even how nice (or not) you are as a person.

A dog loves you as their companion in life's journey, with a simple, no-nonsense, no-conditions commitment. Is it any wonder the word Dog is God spelled backward?

My dogs were there when I came home and soothe my spirit when I am stressed out, over anxious or nervous about something. They detect it, even our sadness and grief. They also wag their tales, smile, lick you hand and face if you let them. Ginger would lie in bed with me and carefully lick the salt off my feet knowing it soothed me. That always helped me fall asleep as a high strung teenager.

There is also a physical benefit to owning as dog. A Dog must be trained, disciplined, and of course walked several times a day. It was a great way to get exercise, but also for me as a priest to get to know the neighborhood around my parish. Training takes patience and perseverance, a tenacity to raise a pup that is good around people. A dog also loves to play fetch, tug of war, and a good wrestle in the grass. All of it, including the walks keeps the owner fairly fit and agile. Yes all of it is easier when we are young, but importantly in our aging it keeps us active and alert. It is a great health addition to my own daily cardio-vascular work outs, weight lifting and bodybuilding. The walks along add 2-3 miles daily to my step count.

Maybe dogs and pets are not for you, they aren't for everyone. But if the readers value nature, an active life-style and plain old companionship- they'll most likely love having a dog.

In retirement I moved from a Rectory with a backyard to a Condo in the sky. My dog and I had to learn a new exercise routine and activity to meet his daily eliminations. It has been a great addition and benefit to my daily cardio work. But even more so, he is my companion as I do those walks. I so look forward to his greeting when I come home as well as a little play-time together. It has reinforced what my parents taught me- that true love is more than just a feeling, it is a commitment. Is that not Jesus' example to me from his sacrifice on the Cross? Committed Love. Love is not sex, or even you make me feel so good. Nor does it make everything perfect. It is commitment. And there are no two ways about it: I'd die for my dog, and he would do the same for me.

Addendum:

When I served on the Commission on Ministry interviewing potential candidates for Holy Orders (Deacons & Priests), I always asked each candidate: "If you were not born a Human Being, what animal would you choose to be and why?" After a few years the Bishop asked me privately why I always asked that question. My answer was brief and to the point. I told the dear Bishop: "My experience as a priest has been that it is not easy to love Human Beings with all our complications. So if the young person cannot express some love of animals or pets, it will be pretty hard for them to do the work of pastoral care, loving Human Beings." To me this is still the most important trait of a good priest- how they love their people and thus the most important trait of those seeking Ordination.

It is interesting to observe that the dog walkers - at the very least -practice some exercise.

I am talking about exercising relieving pain, improving walking, adding healthy years to lives, which are only tangentially mentioned in famous books dedicated to exercising. These books do not mention tenacity, because it would be extremely difficult and costly to experiment for a long period of time if an individual keeps being tenacious.

Therefore, the torch is handed from the writer of the book to the readers, who are totally responsible for introducing exercises into their lives.

Food for thought

1. Would the readers analyze the possibility of increasing the time they walk their dogs?
2. Adding five to ten minutes to walking the dog will improve your exercising time as well as your health, and that of the dog

CHAPTER IX

Avoiding Falls Being Tenacious with Strong Sense of Purpose

"If you associate enough with older people who do enjoy their lives, who are not stored away in any golden ghettos, you will gain a sense of continuity and of the possibility for a full life.
—Margaret Mead

"Courage doesn't always roar. Sometimes courage is the little voice at the end of the day that says I'll try again tomorrow."
— Mary Anne Radmacher

"Courage is not having the strength to go on; it is going on when you don't have the strength."
— Teddy Roosevelt

"FEARLESS is getting back up and fighting for

**what you want over and over again....even though
every time you've tried before you've lost."**
— Taylor Swift

"The groundwork of all happiness is health"
—Leigh Hunt

Relationship between being tenacity and strong sense of purpose

GOING BACK TO the phrase **"sense of purpose".** In this author's book *May Empathy Lead to Sense of Purpose through Tenacity?* on page xii, he cited a very good definition of sense of purpose in Dr. William Damon book's A Path to Purpose, dedicated to analyze this condition on young people, as follows: " sense of purpose is a stable and generalized intention to accomplish something that is — at the same time — meaningful to the self and consequential for the world beyond the self."

In this writer's opinion, although the phrase was basically referred to young people, it is also applicable to any human being, including seniors. It is true that seniors tend to be tired more often than young people. Nonetheless, this author has listed in this book, his own personal case at eighty-two years old, and that of his parents, who died healthily at eighty-eight years of age

Twenty-two famous people who had a very active and useful lives, undoubtedly must have had senses of purpose. Let's list twenty of them in the following table:

Outstanding People's Life Existence in Years

Name	Life existence in years	Name	Life existence in years
Henry Ford	84	Ruth Bader Ginsburg	87
Walt Disney	65	John Marshall	90
Albert Einstein	76	Roger Brooks	83
Socrates	71	Stephen Field	83
Thomas Edison	84	Oliver Wendell Holmes	94
Joseph Stary	68	Louis Brandeis	85
Vincent Van Gogh	47	Charles Evans Hughes	86
Jack London	40	Hugo Lafayette Black	81
Elvis Presley	44	Earl Warren	83
Steven Spielberg	76 (so far)	Franklin Delano Roosevelt	63
Charles Chaplin	88	Dwight D. Eisenhower	78

Summarizing the results of famous peoples' ages: From forty to fifty, 3 / 22= 13.6 %; from sixty-one to seventy 3/22 = 13.6%; from seventy-one to eighty, 4/22= 18.2%, and from eighty-one to ninety-four, 12/22 = 54.5%

All these twenty-two people necessarily must have had senses of purpose; otherwise, they wouldn't have been famous, triumphant, and tenacious.

Therefore, from this table it can be seen as quite possible that people elder than seventy-one years old can have senses of purposes and being tenacious.

It is my opinion that my contribution in writing this book is to awake in elderly people the need for getting better for good if they systematically exercise. From being an activity that — at least temporarily improved their health if they strictly and consistently followed professional instructions — the seniors should introduce them into their normal life for a long time. This is the only way in which PT patients can in fact improve their health issues in the middle and long runs.

The real contribution that this author is trying to explain in this book is that the only way in which elderly people can improve their health, and reduce their probabilities of falling, is to exercise consistently, and making them part of their life.

In his personal case, from November 2020 to July 2022, he has seriously introduced exercising into his life. Having said so, during his last PT sessions, he has: a) improved in just five weeks from walking with a cane pressed on the floor, to walking with a cane always holding it on the floor; b) successfully walking every day at least from 1.5 to 2.5 miles; c) walking turning his head to the right or to the left, upward or downward without losing balance; d) his balance has improved considerably; e) he feels more confident about not falling because his legs are strong; f) after walking systematically, he feels no pain whatsoever in his body.

He is an inspirational speaker, writer, and professor. He feels confident that his example may be followed by some readers of this book.

Believe in yourself, keep exercising and improving your health, don't let procrastination meddle into your health, and remember to stand up after a fall. If you try hard to continue exercising, your improvement will be the best proof to yourself of the convenience of introducing tenacity into your life. In his opinion, procrastination cannot impose its presence in anybody inspired by tenacity.

Read this book, keep it handy, review it whenever the shadow or indolence of procrastination try to interfere with your will and perseverance to exercise.

Food for thought:

1. The readers are suggested to write their own conclusions about this book.

2. Would some readers accept the challenge of writing a summary about the essence of each chapter?

3. Would some readers summarize how they intend to apply the knowledge they have acquired in each chapter, and relate it to their lives after finishing their training sessions with the last professional trainer?

4. Do any readers have any idea about how to be in control of their health by becoming tenacious?

Printed in the United States
by Baker & Taylor Publisher Services